Dance

Contemporary Dance

By Trudy Becker

level 2 little blue readers

www.littlebluehousebooks.com

Little Blue House is distributed by North Star Editions:
sales@northstareditions.com | 888-417-0195

Produced for Little Blue House by Red Line Editorial.

Photographs ©: Shutterstock Images, cover, 4, 13, 15, 21, 24 (top left), 24 (bottom left); iStockphoto, 7, 9, 10, 16, 23, 24 (bottom right); Pexels, 19, 24 (top right)

Library of Congress Control Number: 2022919968

ISBN
978-1-64619-829-0 (hardcover)
978-1-64619-858-0 (paperback)
978-1-64619-913-6 (ebook pdf)
978-1-64619-887-0 (hosted ebook)

Printed in the United States of America
Mankato, MN
082023

About the Author

Trudy Becker lives in Minneapolis, Minnesota. She likes exploring new places and loves anything involving books.

Table of Contents

Showing Emotions

A girl moves her body
slowly, then quickly.
She bursts across the floor.
She stretches her leg out.

A boy pulls his arms into his chest.

Then he jumps up.

He reaches his arms and legs back.

The dancers show the emotions of the music. They are doing contemporary dance.

All About It

Contemporary means happening now. So, contemporary dance is new. But it uses older styles too.

Contemporary
dance uses parts of
modern dance.
It uses parts of ballet too.
It even uses jazz moves.

Dancers use classic forms, but they do their own moves too.

They try to show emotion and tell a story.

Learning How

Contemporary dancers learn many styles. They practice the styles first. Then they can mix them in dances.

They can dance in different ways. Sometimes they dance in groups or pairs, and sometimes they dance alone.

pair

Dancers wear tight but flowing outfits. The clothes show their bodies moving. Sometimes people dance barefoot.

barefoot

Before showtime, dancers get ready.
They put on their outfits and take deep breaths.
It is time for contemporary dance!

Glossary

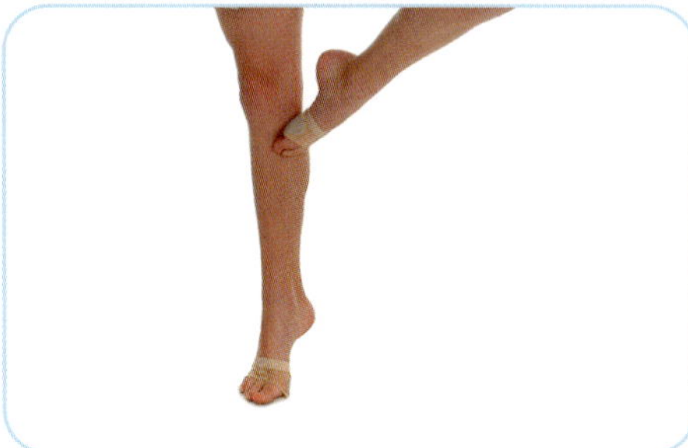

barefoot

pair

outfit

practice

Index